MILLION DOLLAR AUTHOR MINDSET

Sixteen strategies to write your book & build your business

Brett Odgers

Business Growth Advisors

SYDEY, AUSTRALIA

Everyone has a story worth sharing. It's time to share yours.

— BRETT ODGERS

Business Growth Advisors
34 Higginbotham Rd
Gladesville, NSW, 2111
www.milliondollarauthor.global

Book Layout © 2019 Brett Odgers

**Million Dollar Author Mindset – Sixteen strategies to write
your book and build your business** -- 1st ed.
ISBN 978-0-9943007-4-4

ABOUT THE AUTHOR

Husband, father, businessman, keynote speaker, soccer tragic, wanna-be surfer, musician….. And Author

Brett's career arc has been creative, entrepreneurial and fun. After great success as a Photographer and Film Director in his early career, he has gone on to develop a global business consulting practice helping businesses build winning teams and develop inspirational leaders.

He is the founder of the Million-Dollar-Author and the No B.S. Book writing program, which are helping people all over the world write and publish their books. Then build businesses around those books.

CONTENTS

Chapter One

THE IDEA IN BRIEF

Why does it seem to be so difficult to write a book?

One recent survey revealed that up to 85% of adults would like to write a book. Yet a tiny, tiny percentage of them actually complete this lifelong dream of becoming an author. Why is that?

Writing a book is hard, but not complex. It's simpler than you imagine. So why do so few people start?

We work with authors from all over the world helping them write their books, and the thing that's holding most people back from making progress is the way they are thinking about writing a book. Their mindset about becoming an author is a major hurdle.

For hundreds of years we've been shown a model of becoming an author that was based on scarce resources. It's one that's based on the invention of the printing press and the ability to rapidly reproduce printed paper bound up on volumes. Then carefully distributed to discerning customers. This approach was revolutionary hundreds of years ago, and required you to methodically craft your writing, typesetting and printing because it was expensive and difficult to produce printed book.

That meant two things. You had better have an idea worth sharing to a mass audience to make it worthwhile. And you could only afford to print it once so the writing had to be perfect first time

Not surprisingly, the stakes were high if you wanted to share your ideas. The cost was great, the criticism could be widespread and the smallest mistake could mean you pulp the lot and start over again.

It's not your fault that you approach writing books from this perspective, you've been given a broken model. And it's had you thinking about it based on information hundreds of years out of date. Based on a model that is no longer relevant to the digital age. And it's holding you back from sharing your stories to people who would love to hear them and learn from them.

What then do we replace the old thinking with?

We need a new mindset and a new model in order to flourish as an author. And this book outlines how to approach becoming an author today.

A very small percentage of people will become globally famous for their books. Not everyone will become a New York Times bestseller. And that shouldn't stop you from writing and publishing. Narrow your focus, define clearly who you help and how you will help them with your book and you will attract an audience who want your help. It's not about becoming globally famous; It's more about becoming a micro celebrity. If you can be the most important person for your readers, for your niche, then you can develop a meaningful level of celebrity and fame for a narrow readership.

What about making sales? Even the most successful authors find they are not able to replace their wage or salary with book income. Especially in smaller markets like Australia. The dream of income from the book is an old way of thinking as well.

However, income through the book has become an opportunity of immense proportions. Opportunities to develop businesses, book speaking engagements and run workshops are some of the opportunities available when you have written a book. Once you have developed your authority and shred your ideas, you've now earned the right to help people implement this information into their own lives.

The paradigm has now shifted. For the longest time expertise was locked away in learning institutions, such as universities, and the price to unlock that knowledge was high. Exclusive schools have been the keepers of knowledge and the guardians of precious information for a long time.

With the development of worldwide connectivity, globalization has changed the old paradigm and flipped it on its head. knowledge is now freely available worldwide, implementing that knowledge is what people are investing in. Implementation has become the greatest opportunity to produce income from a global audience.

There has ever been a better time in history to write your book. Publishing tools are freely available and printing costs are so low that they are available to everyone. Publishing books is no longer the domain of the aristocratic class, and a global audience is available to all.

It's time to reexamine the old mindsets for becoming an author and build a more useful framework for organizing your ideas, writing your book & sharing your stories.

These 16 mindsets will flip your thinking on how to write your book, create impact & influence with your ideas, and develop income through your book.

Chapter Two

I HATE COLD CALLING

You want me to what!?

Write a book? What about? What for?

I had just informed my business coaching client that I wanted him to write a book to solve his marketing problem.

Alan is a reformed civil engineer who now runs a fire maintenance business in Adelaide, the garden state of Australia. And I've just informed him that I want him to write a book. In fact, I want to make a book the cornerstone of a marketing and sales strategy that is going to completely flip the paradigm for his business.

Alan is a warm, genuine guy, running a family business, who is passionate about protecting his clients from any risk of fire. He really wants to look after people and make sure that they never, ever have to worry about their building burning down. Oh! and I've accidently got him hooked on surfing. But that's a whole other story.

He has a team of 20 people and they cover a large regional city and then a fairly vast regional area. They check extinguishers, maintain complex sprinkler systems and keep all their client's buildings in tip top working order.

By his own admission, this s not sexy work. They don't get the accolades of the heroic firefighters dashing into burning buildings to rescue people. No one is asking Alans team to pose for half naked calendar photoshoots. And the girls aren't dreaming of taking home a fire maintenance guy to meet the parents.

But it's very important work. This team are the preemptive firefighters. In fact, they see it as a failure of epic proportions if a firefighting crew ever have to be called to one of their buildings.

And because it's not sexy it often gets put in the too hard basket, or at least the let's deal with that later basket, for those that have the responsibility for building maintenance. But it's extremely important to get right, lives quite literally depend on it.

To make the job of growing his business a little bit harder, most of his competitors are large national organisations.

In summary. His customers are hard to find, the work he helps them do is something they put off to the last minute, and he is competing against large, large businesses... Oh! And he hates cold calling.

He would steel himself each week to make the call list, internally dreading it. "I know I have to do it and so I just make myself. But I often leave it late, and if any excuse comes up to skip it, I'm happy for the distraction. But I know sooner or later I'll have to make those calls or the business won't survive"

"For my business, or any business that sells a service, to thrive, we need new sales. We need to introduce ourselves to fresh opportunities." Says Alan. Just like any service based business he needs to break into the conversation and introduce himself.

Regular marketing strategies don't seem to have the same impact, they can't find and attract clients that are hard to find. And they can't motivate prospective clients to call you. The consequences of avoiding new business sales for too long could be disastrous. 20 people are reliant on sales for their livelihood. And a dip in sales could mean having to fire someone, or take a cut in pay. There is a gloom that comes over an organisation when you are forced to play, cutting costs anywhere you can, accepting less than perfect clients just to make payroll. It affects everyone. And the thought of that is enough to get most of us doing the thing that is most uncomfortable. Cold calling.

But if you can find great clients, and deliver massive value in your marketing, then you have a sales strategy with the foundations for something really cool. Something fun, something inspirational and inspiring.

Despite the challenges of Alan's niche, he has grown his business this year, put on additional staff and generated additional sales that will represent just under a million dollars in recurring revenue over the next few years.

And he has done that using a strategy that means he never has to cold call ever again. Actually he gets to talk about his favourite subject, you guessed it, fire maintenance, and help people all day long... In between surfing trips that is.

How?

He wrote a book.

His experience told him that the thing most of his clients didn't really understand was how to brief fire maintenance people for quotes and scope of works.

His clients, the strata mangers and building mangers, would rarely be knowledgeable enough about the technical aspects of this subject to be able to expertly compare quotes and proposals. It left them feeling like they may have missed something.

What they really wanted was to feel confident that they would never be left wondering if they did all they could to prevent a building burning down and lives being lost.

So Alan wrote a book to teach his customers, and prospective customers how to think like a fire maintenance engineer.

And it has been very successful, producing hundreds of thousands of dollars of recurring revenue, and helping him find and help his customers be the best they can at their job.

It's not a book you are going to find in a corner bookshop, and it's not going to be on the New York Times bestseller list. But to the people that Alan serves, his book is a much used, much loved companion that helps strata mangers do their jobs and protect people from fire risk.

Then a curious thing happened. Clients started asking if Alan could come and run a workshop, teaching their staff how to do this. Who doesn't love to teach people about something you are excited to talk about? Not is spreading the word and teaching in workshops a great addition to Alans services, it's like having a direct line to the client. Alan is literally teaching his ideal clients the very best industry practice in his field.

So if you were in a training room with a guy who is teaching you, and wrote a book about the process, who then would you turn to when you need a supplier. You turn to the organisation that has demonstrated expertise and authority. And you ask them for help.

In a complete flip, Alans ideal clients are now coming to him, asking for help, and asking for him to tender for the work too. They are not asking just to purchase a product or service; they are asking for help. And in doing so Alan is earning the right to tender for the work.
And he is winning that work.

Instead of selling, he is sharing his expertise.

Instead of cold calling, he is offering a book to help. And instead of dreading the time he has to sit and run through his call list and face the rejections that always comes with cold calling. He is happily answering thoughtful questions and being invited into the training rooms of his ideal clients.

Now a sales meeting is all about how many books did you give away this month, and who did that connect you to.

And he really doesn't have to think about what to include in his content marketing for the month. He has a whole book to draw from.

An increased flow of great enquiries, that are all inbound, from his ideal clients is a dream that he probably didn't think was possible.

Now that he sees the power of becoming a little bit famous to the people that are most important to his business, Alan has come to really enjoy the sales process. Now that he doesn't need to cold call again.

Then only questions now is... What should his next book be about?

If I were to make the crazy suggestion to you of writing a book, what would your topic be? What is the thing that your audience, or ideal clients, need to know that you can help them with?

Alan's book is being used to start a different conversation with his prospective clients. One that is far more valuable than a cold call. To be successful with this strategy it's important that you identify what the problems are that your clients, or readers, have that you can help solve with your expert knowledge. With your book.

If you can frame the problem in a way that connects with your audience, then build a title and topic around that, and provide insight and guidance, then you are starting a conversation at a much deeper level than any sales or marketing brochure.

Chapter Three

A LITTLE BIT FAMOUS

I'd LOVE to write a book but…..

If I had a dollar for every time I'd heard this……
Well, I'd be a rich man.

Because I hear it every. Single. Day.

 Something is holding people back from sharing their
stories and by now I've got a good idea what it is.

This is what people ask me most often.

1. Is what I have to say really valuable to other people? Is my story worth sharing and are my experiences relevant to others?

2. What if I get criticized for my book? Aren't I just opening myself up to be knocked down. What if real experts have a go at me and tell me I've got it wrong.

3. I've seen other people publish a book and it took their careers to higher levels. Can writing a book do that for my career or business? Will it work in my industry? And how do I make money out of it?

4. Where do I even start? I have so many ideas floating around in my head, how do I put that onto paper so that people will want to read it?

5. I'd like to be better known in my industry, because many leaders have written book, but will that make me a target? Am I just making myself a tall poppy?

And here is what they're not telling me, but I know it's on their minds. The fears that creep in whenever anyone considers writing a book.

If I get this wrong I'm concerned that …

- I'll look like an idiot.
- People will criticize me and cut me down to size
- No one will be interested in what I've got to say
- It will be an expensive exercise and I'll end up with a garage full of books that never sell
- It's going to take a long, long time.
- Maybe I really don't know as much as I think.

It's normal to think about all that can go wrong, we wouldn't be human if we didn't. But those instincts for protection are not helping you evolve and grow. They are actually based in evolutionary biology and designed to keep you alive in prehistoric times. They are your fight or flight responses on high alert for threats to your survival. And in our modern age we do not need these instincts to be so vigilant.

On the other hand, if we can overcome the urge to run for our lives, taking a chance on a creative project like this can have wonderful outcomes. If we see the environment for what it is… A safe place where there has never been a better time for creative freedom, and personal expression. Where doing business all over the globe is possible and highly profitable, and where being authentic and genuine and providing great value to others by sharing your experience can give you a significant income, personal freedom and a huge dose of meaning.

If you get it right, a book could open up opportunities for more money, more freedom, and a greater level of impact and influence than you thought possible in your career.

- You'll be able to genuinely call yourself an author, and that's something many people have aspired to.
- All your experience and ideas will be in one place, a book, that you can easily share and sell all over the world.
- It could help a lot of people and have a really positive impact on the world.
- It will create a legacy, something that lives beyond you. Something that you can be proud of.
- It could be the start of something big for your business, because people who are seen as an authority in their field so often get the first choice of projects.
- A book would make a great foundation for marketing and sales of your business or attract attention of bigger career opportunities.
- Building a business that you can run from anywhere in the world is totally possible once you have written your book.

- Speaking engagements, workshops, programs and products are all direct outcomes of capturing your genius and sharing your story in a book.

P.S. It might even make you a little bit famous… At least to the people that are interested in your topic, your business or your career.

Chapter Four

A NEW MODEL FOR SUCCESS AS AN AUTHOR

The million-dollar author model 2.0

Let me introduce you to a completely new way of thinking about using books to build your business, your position as a thought leader and your career.

At the heart of what we do, we help people create million-dollar author businesses. We do that by initially helping our clients to write the book and build business into and around that book.

There are three critical activities to creating a million-dollar author business.

1. Building influence and authority
2. Creating impact and connection through storytelling, and,
3. Producing income by publishing and distributing your books, products and programs.

First we need to create influence.

Influence is when we are seen as an authority in our field. This occurs when we share important information, ideas and expertise, and it helps to position us as an expert. But it's more than an expert, it's someone who is capable of influencing an industry. It's like being a little bit famous.

This is exactly what celebrities manage to do. They use their fam to have influence and opportunity.
When you are seen as an authority people come to you first. If you are seen as an authority in your field it is likely that people will come to you with the best opportunities before they offer it to anybody else.

The second important aspect of becoming million-dollar author is to have impact, to profoundly affect people by sharing your experience your knowledge your stories. This is what impact is all about. And it is affected by how well you tell your stories.

Connecting to your audience through storytelling is a powerful way of creating impact.

Finally, most authors would like to earn income from their ideas. That traditionally comes in the form of books sales. However, there are many other ways of producing income and independence by the becoming a million-dollar author.

Another significant aspect of creating income as an author is the level of freedom it gives you. A new type of freedom that enables you to travel the world, share your ideas, powerfully impact communities, and earn a very good income.

To do that effectively we need to take your ideas and publish them in a way that gives access to your thinking in your methodology to anyone, anywhere in the world.

See image below

The old way of creating a million-dollar author business is slow, laborious and difficult.

In fact, it's so difficult that while we know a huge percentage of people want to write a book, especially if you are a thought leader a senior manager in a big business or you own your own business, a tiny, tiny percentage of people actually complete a book.

A New York Times article recently suggested over 80% of adults wanted to write a book of some form, yet less than 1% of people actually accomplish that goal.

That's because the old way of doing it is broken. It's not your fault because the system was stacked against your success.

We live in a new era where we have can approach becoming an author from a completely different perspective and that's what this book is all about.

We want to show you the new mindset that is required to be successful as an author. And the 16 strategies to help you make that happen. It's simpler and way more fun than the old way. Let me show you the difference between version 1.0 and 2.0.

Influence

In version 1.0 of becoming an author you typically had to demonstrate fairly dry complex data. People often used research and scientific methodology to share their ideas. Unfortunately, it's very difficult to engage people using this approach, and it becomes even more difficult to influence people when you're using complex, dry data in your books.

Version 2.0 of the model that we've developed uses the age old saying that a picture is worth 1000 words.

When you create a visual model for your readers what you're doing is giving them a story, you're giving them context around your ideas as well as content.

It's like creating a map for the data that you're sharing with them. And this is how you can radically change the way people relate to your ideas and expertise.

When you show them the context and you demonstrate how to use your ideas in their lives, your level of influence will increase tenfold.

A mate of mine expresses it like this. When you can articulate the frustrations of your audience and phrase it the way they are in their heads, then you will connect with them as if you're reading their mind.

And when you can read someone's mind and show them the way to solving the problems you will have earned authority status.

Impact

One of the most common questions I get asked is "how do I know my ideas are valuable to other people?" Our experience is that every story is valuable to somebody. And your job is to create stories that are relevant and powerful to your specific readers.

We do this through storytelling. This is one of the most powerful mechanisms for sharing information our culture has ever developed. The ability to tell a story is the ability to transfer your idea directly into the minds and hearts of your readers. So it makes sense to learn how to tell a good story in your own voice. And do that in a way that sounds authentic and congruent and connects with the people it needs to connect with.

In version 1.0 of writing books, the old way really required you to have an extreme story to get the attention of the reading public. For example, if you had survived the disaster or you had an extreme story to tell, publishers really wanted to know who you were and they wanted to find ways to tell that story to as many people as possible.

What it left people feeling was, unless my story is extreme then wasn't worth telling. And that is just not true.

Everybody has stories worth sharing. The readers your book is aimed at, your audience or your niche will be very interested in your story if it helps them improve their lives, their business, their careers. So we no longer need to have extreme stories to be able to have impact with the people that we want to help.

A real, authentic story that shows the way for your readers to overcome the hurdles in their lives will be a very powerful story indeed. The 2nd pillar of version 2.0 is all about finding your voice and finding stories that show people the way.

Income

How do we produce income as an author? Traditional methods of producing income from books is simply through book sales. However there are so many more opportunities to generate income and build businesses through your books. Than simply book sales.

Speaking engagements is a very effective way of building income through your book. Plus there are a multitude of opportunities to develop workshops, online teaching programs and consulting projects once you have written your book.

Version 1.0 of the business of being an author meant

you were forced to look at engaging a publisher to help us put your book together and to sell it. This meant that we needed to pitch our ideas to these publishers.

And if a publisher took you on and you managed to complete your book, for those efforts, the blood sweat and tears of creating a book, you were given a tiny percentage of sales. If you were lucky you received 5% of the cover price of your book.

One of the major reasons to go with the publisher was that they had distribution channels which could put your book in the hands of many, many more people than you could alone.

However now a publisher wants to know how many followers you already have. Or how big is your database is, because they need you to have a significant following before they'll invest in you. It just doesn't look like a good deal to me.

In V2.0 of becoming a successful author we'll show you how to make use of the book to build a wonderful business that is based on sharing your ideas, helping people and producing income from that activity.

The Million Dollar author model

Version 1.0 of becoming an author compared to version 2.0

Chapter Five

THE MINDET OF A MILLION DOLLAR AUTHOR

A no B.S. guide to writing a book to build your business

Writing a book is one of the most intense personal development experiences most of us will experience.

When you pour your ideas, experiences and stories out onto a page you are coming face to face with your demons.

Here are some frameworks that I have found immensely useful in the process of writing your book and building an organisation and a business around the ideas expressed in the book.

These are the 16 strategies for success as an author. The new paradigm to write your book then use it to build your business, your career or to position yourself as a thought leader.

Our Code – The Mindset of a Million Dollar Author				
1	**2**	**3**	**4**	**5**
Progress not Perfection The perfect book doesn't exist. So just make progress toward the best book you can create.	**No Failure, only feedback** When things done work out as planned, see if as valuable feedback. Let's rebrand the word failure	**Don't Take anything personally** From the book The four agreements by Don Miguel Ruiz. This one is important	**This is A book.... Not THE book** This will be one of many. Take it easy on yourself that is your first book.	**Start Calling yourself an author now** The sooner you start identifying as an author the better you will be.
6	**7**	**8**	**9**	**10**
Self-publishing rocks Maximum flexibility is achieved through self-publishing	**Income through books, not from them.** We will focus on how this will build your business. It's about more then royalties and book sales.	**Print on Demand** New technology gives us the ability to do very short runs and be agile with our marketing	**Not for your Peers** This is for the people you are trying to help. Not your peers. So you can ignore their well-intentioned advice	**Write for One Person** When you can communicate like you are talking to one person. It's powerful. Write for a single person
11	**12**	**13**	**14**	**15**
Write like you talk Write as if you are having a wonderful conversation with a good friend over coffee. It will sound authentically like you	**Tell them everything** Don't hold anything back. Leave it all out on the field. They'll pay you to implement. Knowledge is freely available	**Deadlines are your friend** If you find you are too busy to write. Set a deadline and declare it publically. There is no better motivator	**Building Cathedrals.** Take the long view. You aren't building a wall, you are building a cathedral	**Batteries Included** People who come with batteries included make great authors. Take responsibility for your progress
16 Models and frameworks The old way of writing books is difficult because the model is no longer relevant. With the right frameworks you can write a book				

Download a copy of the worksheet here.
https://www.dropbox.com/s/qatvhedjbn2f282/M
indsets of a million dollar author.pdf?dl=0

Strategy 1. Progress Not Perfection

Perfection is a myth. And it's a destructive myth.
The war cry of "But I'm a perfectionist" is just setting people up for disappointment. Perfect stories, perfect grammar, perfect book title, perfect spelling. It's not helpful.

Surfers are on an endless search for the perfect wave. Sports people are searching for the perfect technique; entrepreneurs are searching for the perfect product or marketing campaign. It' doesn't exist. and even if you managed to get it perfect, it's only for a tiny fleeting moment.

Unless you embrace the search and the journey and acknowledge that there will never be perfection you are missing out on the joy of creativity, of exploration and experience.

The famous world war two Allied General, George Patton, famously said. "An imperfect plan violently executed right now, is better than a perfect plan next week"

My version of that goes like this....
An imperfect book, thoughtfully & enthusiastically executed right now, is better than the perfect book next year.

Strategy 2. No failure only feedback

It's time re rebranded our mistakes.
And called them what they are.... Feedback, not fail-
ures.

Nature is imperfect by design, and most of the great
discoveries have happened by accident. One of the
most exciting visual innovation in my career as an
advertising photographer and film maker was the ad-
vent of Cross pressed film. The colours of this process
were vibrant, different and absolutely alluring. And
even ad agency was begging us to use the technique
for their campaigns.

And it all came about by mistake.

Back in the days of film photography and cinematog-
raphy there were two different chemical processes
used to develop the film. E6 produced the transparency films which were used on high end commercial
shoots. This is also the film used to make the old
slides your uncle Arthur showed you of his trip to
Greece. And the remainder of the world used nega-
tives and prints, which used a chemical process called
C-41.

One day someone mixed up the films and put them in the wrong process line. They took the Colour negative film that was intended to be processed in C-41 chemistry and accidentally ran it thought the colour transparency process called E-6.

The result was all wrong… And completely brilliant.

A new technique was born. It was called Cross Processing. And in your phone right now is a filter called Dramatic or Cross processed that emulates this effect.

We refined the process and film selection it so that the results were predictable and repeatable. And in high demand. My studio completed many, many campaigns using this process. That was at first considered a mistake.

The world of science, art & medicine is also littered with examples like this. Countless times the results of a mistake have pushed our thinking way beyond and into innovative and highly disruptive techniques, methods and technologies.

How about we take the perspective that when something doesn't go as planned we ask ourselves, what is there to learn in this. What's the feedback telling me? Because that's where innovation lives. In the ability to draw insights out of feedback. Especially when things don't go as planned.

Strategy 3. Don't take anything personally

One of my favourite book is called the 4 agreements by Don Miguel Ruiz. He is a Mexican author and outlines 4 agreements as a practical guide for personal freedom.

You'd think by the title it's a little bit woo-woo (read, spiritual and perplexing). But actually it's deeply practical and offers a true insight into how to make better choices.

The 2nd agreement is particularly important for you as an author, and entrepreneur. (it doesn't matter whether you are a social entrepreneur or commercial entrepreneur).

It simply says "Don't take anything personally"
Don Miguel describes it so much better than I can in his book where he says.

"Whatever happens around you, don't take it personally... Nothing other people do is because of you. It is because of themselves. All people live in their own

dream, in their own mind; they are in a completely different world from the one you [sic] live in. When we take something personally, we make the assumption that they know what is in our world, and we try to impose our world on their world.

Even when a situation seems so personal, even if others insult you directly, it has nothing to do with you. What they say, what they do, and the opinions they give are according to the agreements they have in their own minds...Taking things personally makes you easy prey for these predators. They can hook you easily with one little opinion and feed you whatever poison they want, and because you take it personally, you eat it up....

The Author goes on to apply this rule even to his own thoughts.

Even the opinions you have about yourself are not necessarily true; therefore, you don't need to take whatever you hear in your own mind personally...Don't take anything personally because by taking things personally you set yourself up to suffer for nothing....When we really see other people as they are without taking it personally, we can never be hurt by what they say or do. Even if others lie to you, it is okay. They are lying to you because they are afraid.

There is a huge amount of freedom that comes to you when you take nothing personally. You become immune to black magicians, and no spell can affect you regardless of how strong it may be. The whole world can gossip about you, and if you don't take it personally you are immune. Someone can intentionally send emotional poison, and if you don't take it personally, you will not eat it. When you don't take the emotional poison, it becomes even worse in the sender, but not in you.

As you make a habit of not taking anything personally, you won't need to place your trust in what others do or say. You will only need to trust yourself to make responsible choices. You are never responsible for the actions of others; you are only responsible for you. When you truly understand this, and refuse to take things personally, you can hardly be hurt by the careless comments or actions of others.

If you keep this agreement, you can travel around the world with your heart completely open and no one can hurt you. You can say, "I love you," without fear of being ridiculed or rejected. You can ask for what you need."

I LOVE this idea because whether you are leading or surrendering to your creativity, others will often have a lot to say about your efforts.

> *What this 2nd agreement teaches me is that whatever people say... it's not about me, my book or my creative output. It's about them.*

Their comments are about them. Their fears, their jealousies, their own perception of life. It's got very little to do with me.

What I've found is that the most brilliant people that I've met don't seem to have the need to prove how brilliant they are. And if you challenge their ideas they don't take it personally. They don't arc up and start a fight. Because they are infinitely curious about alternative perspectives, and always open to different points of view because it might just tie into a question they've been grappling with. I usually walk away feeling valued and included in these interactions. A generous abundance has just taken place.

On the other hand, I've met many people who are desperate to prove how clever they are. Just waiting for a gap in the conversation to show you how superior they are and conversely how inferior you are. If you buy into this, you'll end up feeling diminished by the interaction.

As Don Miguel says. See it for what it is. It's a reflection of their reality, not yours. And has nothing to do with you, your book or your ideas. It has everything to do with the choices they have made about how they see the world.

Again. The choice is yours.

I highly recommend you get a printed copy of this book. The audio book is awesome too. Here is a link to where you can find it.
https://www.amazon.com/Four-Agreements-Practical-Personal-Freedom/dp/1878424319

Strategy 4. This is "A Book"… Not "The Book"

The book you are about to write will not be the only book you publish. In fact, it will be the first of many books you complete.

That seems like a far-fetched idea right now, but every person I know who stared out to write a single book has ended up writing many more.

Because it's difficult to contain all the ideas in one single volume once you get started. It's useful to think of this as the beginning of your journey as an author

In one of my recent books I fully embraced this and told readers that there was much more to the topic I was discussing that I could cover in a single chapter or a single book. And mentioned that this would be expanded in the next book. I even had a reader ask… So when's the next book coming out that you mentioned in this book?

This idea gives you a bit of a break when it comes to completing the first book, and supports the above idea. Progress not perfection. You don't have to make your first book your magnum opus. It's the beginning of the journey for you.

As you gain skills in developing books and book ideas you'll find that it takes less and less time to produce a book. Many people are writing a book a year as their business grows. As they grow their business as a million-dollar author they develop new depth and techniques to help their audience. And rather than repeat themselves over and overt it makes sense to produce another book about the subject.

There is another interesting effect here to talk about. And it's the relationship between the number of pages in your book and the number of people who fully read it. Studies have shown that if your book is over 200 pages in length, only 3% of people will read it all the way through. If it's over 300 pages that number drops to 1%.

However, if your book is under 65 pages in length over 80% of people will read it all the way through.

What that equates to is that if your book is approximately the length that someone to read on a 2 - 4 hours' plane journey then you have a high chance of sharing all your ideas. That's a great argument for taking your ideas and publishing them in smaller, easily digestible chunks of information. Just like this book. It's only part of the picture, but it's a very important element.

Strategy 5. Start calling yourself an author right now.

And start telling your friends and colleagues that you are writing a book. It's great accountability, because they are going to ask you how you are going with it regularly.

It's the beginning of a shift in your perspective of yourself.

Most people think an author is someone who has sold millions of brook and had the novel made into a movie. But millions of authors don't have that experience.

If you are writing a book, whether it's finished or not, you are an Author. Embrace that fact and test it out by putting author on your business card and telling people you are an author.

You are going to want to have an answer for the next question your friends will ask. What are you working on?

Because if you don't have a good answer for that it will be the only question you are going to get asked by your friends, especially if you are English or Australian, we are famous for that.

You may not know that in the first part of my career I was a film director and photographer. And early on I attended a 2-day film school with a very famous American film producer.

Because he is famous people want to connect with him at parties and functions. They'd like to be included in his next project.

So he asks them. What do you do? And this is their most common reply.

I'm working in the props department right now but what I really want to do is be a director.
Or
I just took any job I could get, which is in the catering van right now, but I really want to be a director of photography, a cinematographer.

They tell him what they are doing now and what their hopes and dreams for their ideal job is. So what does he hear? I work in props dept., or catering.

He knows that the chances of starting in props, working your way through the ranks before progressing to the lighting dept. and working your way through those ranks before moving to the camera dept. and finally to become a director is a million to one shot.

Probably 10 million to 1. So wherever you are now is likely to be where you'll end up.

The solution. Start calling yourself what you want to be. In this case a director. In your case, an Author.

He posed the question. If you want to be a director, why don't you tell people you are a director?

But, ahhhh,…. I'm working in the props dept. right now. And I haven't directed a Hollywood movie.

Sure, but I'll bet you've directed a few things. Student films, stuff for your own show reel. If you are really lucky you may have even had a few small commercial or corporate jobs that paid money. So why don't you call yourself a director now?

This famous producer suggests it's because you're afraid of the next question. So what are you working on right now?

And you'll have to admit that you aren't working on some blockbuster that they've heard of. And you'll be seen as a failure.

Here is the answer he says big-time Hollywood directors respond with.

"I'm working on a number of projects right now that are in various stages of production."

Some are in the scripting phase, some in casting, others are in shooting and I even have a few in post-production.

You know what, even a student director could respond in exactly the same way as a Hollywood director and it would be completely true. They may not be Hollywood blockbusters or even paid jobs, but everyone who aspires to be a director is working on a script, trying to convince their friends to act in their latest short film. They are likely shooting something, and late at night editing another project or putting music to a scene.

So why not tell people you are a director?

If I asked Seth Godin, or any other big name highly paid, prolific author what they are doing right now I'll bet his answer would be similar. Well I've got a number of projects that are in various stages of production right now. I'm developing a new book idea, and finishing the cover design and printing on my current book. At the same time I'm promoting the book I completed last year and running a consultancy proactive based on the ideas in the book I wrote 10 years ago.

> *It's time to call yourself what you are. An Author and an entrepreneur.*

And use this answer for the very next question. (which is what are you working on right now)

"I've got a number of projects that I'm working on in various stages of production. The one I'm most excited about is the book I'm writing on [insert your subject here]. It helps [inset your niche here] by teaching them how to [insert your outcomes here].

For example, if you ask me about the book you are reading right I might respond like this.

The book I'm most excited about right now is called Million Dollar Author. It helps coaches and consultants to capture their ideas and experiences into a compelling book, self-publish it, and build a million-dollar business around it.

When are you going to try this out next?

Strategy 6. Self-Publishing gives more flexibility than going with a publisher

The dream of handing over your manuscript to a publisher and having them do all the design, printing, distribution and marketing work of making your book successful is exactly that. A dream.

Andrew Griffiths is a very successful Australian author and entrepreneur with more than 11 books sold in over 50 countries he knows a thing or two about the book business. He tells me that when he handed over his first book to his publishers he was shocked to find out that they expected him to get out and market and sell the book.

The point at which I decided to become a self-publisher was when I discovered that if I wanted to give away books to my clients, friends, family or at speaking engagements, I would have to buy the books at retail price from the publisher, or maybe with a little discount. MY OWN BOOK. In reality, it wouldn't really be my own book at that stage. It would be theirs.

On the other hand, what I needed was...

Someone to edit my book. Easily sourced from a worldwide market now.

A book cover design, again designers from a global marketplace are now available from my keyboard.
Publishers bits and pieces such as ISBN numbers and bar codes. Simple when you know how.
A way to distribute my book globally via an online book store, gather income from book sales. Oooh, that was looking like a challenge.

And finally someone to print my book at a reasonable cost per unit. About $4-6AUD per book it turns out.

Then turn it into a kindle and audio book as well. This too is available to everyone who has a laptop or a child at high school, if you can get them away from the latest game to help you.

I was happy to market and distribute it locally and do the PR and sales through my existing business systems and lots of automation.

Turns out every element of that is available as a self-publisher tool from great organisations who are only too happy to help you.

Benefits of going with a publisher???? Not many in my experience.

And the process will be quicker more flexible. You'll have greater control and far better opportunities to use the book creatively after it's complete.

> *It turns out self-publisher tools are freely available from great organisations who are only too happy to help you.*

Strategy7. Income thorough the book, not from book sales

We've all heard the story of an unemployed J.K. Rowling who wrote Harry potter in cafe's between dropping her daughter off to schools. And goes onto to become a billionaire creator of several book series, movie franchises and theme parks.

That's a great story of making money from the book. And it represents such a tiny, tiny, tiny percentage of the writing population that it's closer to a fairytale than a pathway forward. The average non-celebrity author, like you and me, would stand to make an average of about $20k from book sales if they are quite successful. If you are in a bigger market like the US, it might be more like $80k - $100k. It's a surprisingly small amount of money to make from such a huge effort of writing a book, which in some cases take years.

I want you to focus instead on building business through the book. And what I mean by that is to create programs, workshops, apps and businesses from the implementation of your ideas from the book. To give you an example. Most non-fiction authors are capable of building a Million Dollar a year revenue through the business that come from the book. And this approach results are much more achievable and predictable method than hoping a movie studio find your book and turns it into a film franchise.

And the results eclipse the earnings from book sales alone.

To get any results from a publishing deal, you'll first have to put up some money yourself. It will take quite a long time for the publisher to edit and design the book so they fell it will stand out omg book shelves. You will get the satisfaction of seeing your book in airports and book stores. But that's a fairly fleeting send of achievement.

Building a business that positively impacts the lives of many people. And which generates a good income, while giving you the autonomy and freedom to do work that is meaningful and leaves a legacy. And that's a way cooler level of satisfaction than seeing your books at the airport in my opinion

Strategy 8. Print on demand means you can make quick and inexpensive changes.

Gone are the days when you had to print 10,000 copies of your book to make it financially feasible. And if you found a spelling error in the book you were stuck with a lot of copies.

Now we have print on demand services from big reputable suppliers like Amazon and Ingram Spark. This gives you the ability to print one single copy if you like. And it gives stores like Amazon the ability to not have to stock large volumes of niche products like specialty books.

What that means as an author is that you can print a small run of books, send it around to friends and trusted advisors for feedback. And if changes need to be made, then it's very simple. Upload the new file, and print the next run.

One of my recent books was about of a young team of soccer players in their quest to build a winning team. When some of the parents read it they felt that, despite not using their full name and mostly using their nicknames, it was still possible for someone to identify their sons. The last thing I wanted to do was upset anyone, and it was simple to change the name of the club, and the players throughout the entire book so that there was no way any of the people could be identified. A new ISBN number, and new print run probably cost me less than $80.

I was actually receiving a lot of very positive feedback about the book in the first 6 months, and some readers were writing to me to let me know what an impact the team culture ideas from the book was making in their teams. So I took advantage of the ability to update the book and included the reader's experiences at the end of some of the chapters. This gave great social proof to the book and connected their readers to more than just ideas, it connected them to actions and results.

This time I didn't even have to get a new ISBN number. Just added a few pages, re-uploaded the file and did another print run.

Another example of using the mindset of progress not perfection.

Strategy 9. This book is not for your peers.

Most of the demons in your head come from the expected reactions and criticisms of your peers. They'll discover I'm really an imposter. I don't know as much about this as I thought and I'll be found out. Or someone will challenge me and I'll look like an idiot.

The perspective I'd encourage you to take is that this is not for your peers, it's actually for the audience you want to help. And as a mate of mine reminds me often." In the land of the blind, a one eyed man is king". In other words, this book is for the people who are not your peers, and need your help. Your experiences and stories are going to make a great impact on someone. probably not your peers. They are likely to tell you all the reasons why this book isn't uncovering any new ground, while under the surface they'll be wishing they had written their book.

Your book is not for your peers, it's for your community who are dead keen for your help

James Morrison is one of the top three trumpeters in the world. He grew up quite close to me and we performed in the same local musical productions when I was young, and we marveled at his talent. he seemed to have a special something. Many years later I'd find out exactly what that something was. James has gone on to have a stellar career as a musician, released many albums, countless performances and collaborations.

One day I found myself sitting in a corporate workshop in a small group talking to James about why people come to see him play.

He posed the question to the group. "Why do you think people come to see me play" A participant chimed in. because you are the best trumpet player in the world. Clearly quite pleased with her answer. James quietly shook his head. Nope, that's not it.

We were all puzzled. But he went to say. "there are only three or maybe four other trumpet players in the world who really know whether what I was playing is, in fact, the world class. And most of my audience members have no idea whether I'm playing at the top of my game or just phoning it in. So that's not it".

He sat forward in his chair, lowered his voice, and in a bit of a conspiratorial manner let us in on the secret.

People come to see me play because I'm having such a great time on stage, playing my music, jamming with my band mates that the enjoyment is infectious.

People come to see how much joy I get from my music, and they get to share a little bit of that joy too".

I think that's true of many musicians and performers. I'm a guitarist in a rock band on weekends. And I can tell you that we all worry about playing the songs flawlessly. But if we are having a great time with each other, and being totally present with the music and the audience, that sense of fun is one of the most infections things I've ever seen. Having a great time playing music together is so important to a performance, that if we totally screw up a song, maybe miss the 2nd verse completely, the audience will not notice the mistake. What they notice is the energy, creativity and passion that is put into the show.

On the other hand, I've witnessed bands play a song flawlessly, perfect guitar solos, singers that are pitch perfect, drums that are right every time... And it has no soul. they are so focused on being flawless for their musical peers that they forget why they are there. To entertain and engage the audience and share a little of the joy we experience with them.

Your job as an author is to share a little of your joy with your audience. Not play perfectly for your peers.

Strategy 10. Write for one person

In Marketing there is an interesting concept called an audience of one. What that means is when creating an advertising campaign know who you are creating it for and create a message that speaks to that person. The reason it's such a powerful idea is that when you know who your audience is and can really get inside their heads, you end up speaking a universal truth that touches many, many people.

When you are writing your book get to know who your audience is, understand their pain and share your experience of dealing with that pain. Then create a bridge for them, give them a clear bright future and share how you crossed over to the other side of that bridge.

Strategy 11. Write like you talk.

Aaron Sorkin is one of the most talented screenwriters of his age. He is known for writing movies such as The Social Network, The American President, and Molly's Game, and television shows like The West Wing and The Newsroom. They are all filled with optimism, brilliant dialogue and a hopefulness that I find completely mesmerizing.

For such a brilliant writer he is more difficult to listen as he talks because his mind is running at a million miles an hour in a number of directions. I was watching him talk recently when a moment of clarity sprang from his mouth. "People tell you there are rules to writing. But that's a lie. There are no rules, we are all just making it up as we go".

One of the authors on my book writing program was astonished when she published her book that readers responded with comments that they liked her own stories and experiences more than they like the interviews and case studies of far more famous and successful people. I believe that this is because you are writing like you would speak to someone. You are connecting with your own story and humbly offering it to others. So take some comfort from a highly successful author like Aaron Sorkin and know that there are no rules to writing. There is just your voice and your story. So embrace it and write like you would if you were having a really great conversation with a friend over a coffee.

P.S. Aaron Sorkin goes onto to elaborate that if there were any rules to writing the only rule book is Aristotle's Poetics. Just as in music it outlines some basics, time signature, what key the piece is etc. But how you play the game within those boundaries is entirely up to you.

Make your writing conversational, not formal. And for that reason many authors are now speaking out their book rather than sitting at a keyboard and typing it out. If you are someone who learns or processes information by talking, then this method may be a great option for you. Simply recording yourself talking out a chapter, then having it transcribed is a very fast and effective way to make progress, and capture the conversational tone of your writing.

One of the authors on my No. B.S. book writing program has found that if she creates an email to herself on her phone, then hits the little microphones button and dictates, she is able to create chapters very fast. And capture her conversational, intimate style. She then emails it to herself, which gives her a backup copy of everything she writes as well.

Strategy 12. Tell them everything

How much should you give away in your book. If you are wanting people to pay you to work with them does giving away all the secrets mean they'll just read the book and not employ your organisation?

I've read more than a few books that spend a lot of time telling us all the problems, doing a great job of ratcheting up the level of pain and discomfort in the reader and just was you are about to turn the page for the answer to this pain…. The author holds back. Worse still they only offer the solution if you join their program. Aarrggghh. That drives me crazy and totally destroys trust in the author. I feel manipulated and the chances of me parting with money to work with someone like this is very low. Because they are stringing me along in a piece of sleazy marketing rather than an insightful and compelling book.

There are two theories that are impacting us here. One is the rule of scarcity, and the other is the law of Abundance.

__The Rule of Scarcity__ suggests that says that there is are finite resources in the world and if you don't get your fair share of them someone else will take away what's yours. Scarcity plays a large role in the persuasion process. … The more scarce an item, the more the item increases in value, and the greater the urge to own it. Whenever choice is limited or threatened, the human need to maintain a share of

*the limited commodity and it makes us crave it
even more.*

If you approach writing your book with a scarcity
mindset then you'll tend to think people are going to
steal your ideas, and use them to get as much as they
can. To advantage themselves while leaving you out
of the equation. It's a very popular framework of
thinking and plays into our fears. We can see it everywhere, and one of the most salient examples at the
moment is in American politics under the leadership
of president Donald Trump. If we don't protect what's
ours, others will take it away. That's scarcity thinking. And it creates an unnecessary competitive and
destructive set of behaviours.

> *Steven Covey, the author of The Seven Habits
> of Highly Effective People, coined the term
> **Abundance mentality** in his 1989 best-selling
> book. It's a concept where people believe that
> there are enough resources and success for
> everyone. That success for one of us creates
> success for all of us.*

In the scarcity mindset if someone wins it means others lose. But doesn't give any consideration to the fact
that so often when someone else wins or is successful

in a situation, that others win also. It's captured in the axiom 'A rising tide floats all boats"

I encourage you to take the abundant approach to writing your book. Help others win by telling them everything, don't hold anything back. And by doing that you'll help others win and that intern will help you win.

Choose abundance.

The other major factor is that in the age of ubiquitous information knowledge is no longer scarce or the domain of only a privileged few. Information is everywhere and available at nearly zero cost to anyone who cares to go searching. Whatever knowledge you think you have total ownership over in your book is likely available somewhere else.

But what people cannot find elsewhere is the implementation of that knowledge. And that's highly valuable.

Give freely of your knowledge and people will come to you for help implementing that information into their lives.

Strategy 13. Too Busy. Set a deadline.

Parkinson's law states that work will expand to fill the time available for its completion. In other words people will usually take all the time allotted, and frequently more, to complete a task.

If you have to complete a task before leaving for an overseas flight at 5pm. It's going to get done... by 5pm.
If on the other hand you have no deadline or you have weeks to complete it. guess what. It's going to take weeks to complete.

The moral of this tale. Set yourself a firm deadline. Declare it publicly and your brain's need for congruency will take care of the rest. Congruency is your brains insatiable need to align your behaviour with your internal beliefs. So if you declare a deadline you are going to feel a bit uncomfortable internally until you meet that commitment.

In many creative endeavors a brilliant strategy is to create a deadline, maybe even assign a consequence to not meeting it, and let nature do the rest.

"I'm not going to have a drink until the book is finished" Declared Chris. This is no small thing because Chris lives in the Australian outback where life revolves around having a beer with friends and popping a cork occasionally. But creating a deadline with a consequence helped remind him of the urgency of finishing his book.

Let me introduce you to a really, really radical idea. Wouldn't it be cool if you could write your book in 4 hrs. and publish it in 4 days? Well that's exactly how I produced this book that you are reading right now.

I set a truly mad deadline to see if I could have a finished product within a week. I focused on one aspect of writing books, which is the mindsets required for success when becoming an author. I created a framework to get it done in that period of time and got it finished. Total time writing. Less than 4 hrs. Production, cover and publishing time was a few days. With a goal of a finished book within a week it helped me only focus on what will get that job done.

Strategy 14. You are building a cathedral.

Have you ever been to the famous Parisian cathedral Notre Dame? It's over 800 years old and it's totally awe inspiring.

As I was walking around it recently I couldn't help but visualize Napoleon being crowned emperor of France and snubbing the Pope at the same time. Or Joan of arc being executed just meters from where I stood. Or the engineering marvel of the flying buttresses that made the grand span of the church possible.

Momentous events in history occurred inside these walls that have stood through so many centuries.

And when the walls of this cathedral were being built the workers shed blood sweat and tears over its construction.

I'm reminded of a story that the Author Simon Sinek told in his 2010 book Start with Why.

"Consider the story of two stonemasons. You walk up to the first stonemason and ask, "Do you like your job?" He looks up at you and replies, "I've been building this wall for as long as I can remember. The work is monotonous. I work in the scorching hot sun all day. The

stones are heavy and lifting them day after day can be backbreaking. I'm not even sure if this project will be completed in my lifetime. But it's a job. It pays the bills." You thank him for his time and walk on.

About thirty feet away, you walk up to a second stonemason. You ask him the same question, "Do you like your job?" He looks up and replies, "I love my job. I'm building a cathedral. Sure, I've been working on this wall for as long as I can remember, and yes, the work is sometimes monotonous. I work in the scorching hot sun all day. The stones are heavy and lifting them day after day can be backbreaking. I'm not even sure if this project will be completed in my lifetime. But I'm building a cathedral."

WHAT these two stonemasons are doing is exactly the same; the difference is, one has a sense of purpose. He feels like he belongs. He comes to work to be a part of something bigger than the job he's doing. Simply having a sense of WHY changes his entire view of his job. It makes him more productive and certainly more loyal. Whereas the first stonemason would probably take another job for more pay, the inspired stonemason works longer hours and would probably turn down an easier, higher-paying job to stay and be a part of the higher cause. The second stonemason does not see himself as any more or less important than the guy making the stained glass windows or even the architect. They are all working together to build the cathedral. It is this bond that creates camaraderie. And that camaraderie and trust is what brings success. People working together for a common cause."

This idea highlights a profound element of writing your book. You aren't just laying bricks; you are building a cathedral. Sometimes that work will be back breaking, difficult and challenging. So keep a sense of why you are doing this in your mind. Keep a vision of who you are helping, who you want to lead to more abundance clearly in your mind. Because that's going to make all the difference when you are finding the work hard.

And if you are fortunate enough this book will stand for many years and leave a legacy for others to enjoy.

Strategy 15. Batteries included

When opened your Christmas presents as a kid, and saw that it was the most brilliant new toy. After ripping open the packaging you discovered that it needed batteries to fire it up. Frantically you searched the box for those magic words..... Batteries included.

Thanks goodness. Install them and you were good to go. Happiness was all consuming.

If on the other had it didn't have batteries included the chances were pretty low that you would be getting much Christmas joy that day, because there is nowhere to buy batteries on Christmas morning.

Some people come with batteries included, and others constantly need someone else to plug into for energy. What makes a successful author is that you come with batteries included.

If you are one of those people that need to search around for batteries before you can get started on anything, then becoming an author may not be for you. It requires you to be a self-starter. It means that the responsibility for motivation is yours alone.

Motivation is helped by staying focused on the big picture, the bright future. And your compelling reason for striving toward that. That's your batteries.

Strategy 16. Models are maps

If a picture is worth a thousand words, then why not paint a picture.

One of the essential elements of writing a book is that it helps unpack your ideas so that you can share them and explain them to others. People who are trained in journalism and writing are particularly good at using them to create vivid experiences. The rest of us have to do the best we can.

One of the very best tools for doing that is to create models, frameworks and visual pictures to help embed the knowledge in your reader's mind. And provide a framework for them to understand difficult concepts, then relate it to others.

Imagine you are climbing a ladder. You start at the first rung, and slowly progress to the next rung.. That's a lot like….insert your process here.

I just created a metaphor and provided a framework for you to understand it quickly. Because you know what a ladder is. That's a model.

And it doesn't need to be fancy or clever. You simply need to create a picture in your readers mind.

A pyramid, a triangle a Venn diagram or square divided into quadrants, they are all pictures that you can use to visualize your data.

Make models out of everything you do. Include them in your book and talk to them. That's exactly what I did in chapter 4 of this book. I created a simple model explaining the difference between the old way of achieving success as an author and the new way. Now you have a model for understanding at a glance, what is actually quite a complex idea.

Chapter Six

START YOUR OWN BOOK NOW

Is it O.K. if I be your book writing coach for a moment?

It's time for you to take action.

It's time to work out what the very next step is. And here's my strong advice. Make it simple.

So what are your top 3 insights from reading this book? Write them below

My top three insights are

1.

2.

3.

What project do you now know you need to work on in the next 30 days?

What are 3 simple actions you can take to make progress on that project. Make the first action so easy you can get it done in the next 10 mins.

1.

2.

3.

Chapter Seven

HOW CAN I GET HELP WRITING MY BOOK?

The 4-Hour book writing program

Is it possible to write a book in 4 hours? That's the question I posed my team? Because the major hurdle for most people who want to write a book is having time to do the writing. Could we really create a system so that anyone could create a valuable non-fiction book that explores one area of a subject in detail? In publishing terms it's called a Monograph, but when it's in the hands of the people you want to reach… It's just called a book.

The answer is yes. The book you've just read was created using our 4-hour method. And we now have authors from all over the world publishing their books in weeks rather than months. Using our templates and frameworks, our team structure your thinking so your book is focused and valuable. During our Authors interviews we download all your content, our editors clean up the language and format the manuscript into a book. You have a chance to edit, delete or expand & amplify on some ideas, while our team design a book cover, register it for libraries & online booksellers, add identifiers and set you up on our publishers portal ready for sale on Amazon and other international book platforms. We'll also create a basic e-book that can be used in digital marketing.

If you want to author a book that will help you create impact, authority and income but don't have the time to write, then this program was built for you.

http://4hourbook.pages.ontraport.net/welcome

The No. B.S. book writing program

The No. B.S. book writing program has people from all over the world joining together to write & publish their books.

This program is for you if you know that writing a book will help you and your business and want insight, guidance and inspiration to make your book real and get it published.

You'll probably have a jumble of ideas running around in your head and need help identifying what to write about, how to structure it and then develop your ideas and stories to give it impact. Plus, a world of shortcuts, templates and frameworks to make your book a reality.

It may be your first book or your next book, but we've had great success helping people from Australia, Europe, America, Asia, New Zealand and Africa become published authors.

Our unique approach helps you build business through your book even before it's finally published.

The program is not for you if you are writing a novel. That's not our genius zone. But if you have a career or a business that would benefit by sharing your ideas and building authority then this is the place to be.

The Million Dollar Author Program

The Million Dollar Author program is for those that have a book and want to build a million-dollar business around it.

Developing programs, and enhancing marketing and sales are some of the massive benefits of writing a book and creating an Authority marketing strategy

Ultimately most people on this program are building four things in their lives

- More time freedom in their lives
- Greater impact and influence
- More income from multiple sources
- And a deep level of meaning in their work

You'll join other business owners and authors from all over the globe to build your million-dollar author business.

The four areas we focus on to do this are…

.

1. Creating world class intellectual property through storytelling techniques that powerfully influence.
2. Finding your voice and telling stories that create impact

3. Creating an ecosystem of programs, products and services

4. Clearly understanding the needs, frustrations and goals of your audience.

Free Resources

www.4hourbook.pages.ontraport.net/welcome

www.nobsbookwritingcourse.pages.ontraport.net

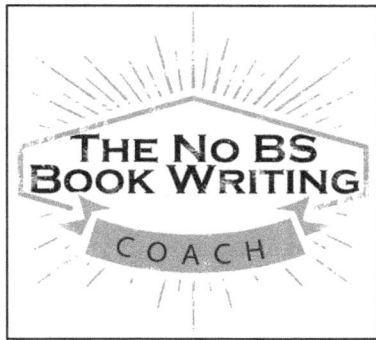

Watch Author case study interviews here.

Case Study 1. Christchurch - N.Z.

www.nobsbookwritingcasestudy.pages.ontraport.net/Ajohnston

Case Study 2 Sydney - Australia

www.nobsbookwritingcasestudy.pages.ontraport.net/sfrankland

Case Study 3 Istanbul – Turkey

https://www.youtube.com/watch?v=rugIDefWegc

www.ingramcontent.com/pod-product-compliance
Lightning Source LLC
Chambersburg PA
CBHW030533210326
41597CB00014B/1131